SCHIRMER'S LIBRARY OF MUSICAL CLASSICS

Vol. 2129

T0088794

SELECTED PIANO MASTERPIECES

INTERMEDIATE LEVEL

47 Pieces by 16 Composers

ISBN 978-1-4950-8801-8

G. SCHIRMER, Inc.

DISTRIBUTED BY
HAL•LEONARD®

www.schirmer.com
www.halleonard.com

CONTENTS

CARL PHILIPP EMANUEL BACH
7   March in G Major, BWV Appendix 124

JOHANN SEBASTIAN BACH
8   Invention No. 1 in C Major, BWV 772
10   Invention No. 2 in C minor, BWV 773
12   Invention No. 4 in D minor, BWV 775
14   Invention No. 8 in F Major, BWV 779
16   Prelude in C Major from *The Well-Tempered Clavier*, Book. 1, BWV 846
18   Prelude in C minor, BWV 999
20   Bourée from Lute Suite No. 1 in E minor, BWV 996

LUDWIG VAN BEETHOVEN
21   Six Variations on a Swiss Song, WoO 64

JOHANN FRIEDRICH BURGMÜLLER
24   La chasse (The Chase) from *25 Easy and Progressive Studies*, Op. 100, No. 9
26   L'adieu (The Farewell) from *25 Easy and Progressive Studies*, Op. 100, No. 12
28   Consolation from *25 Easy and Progressive Studies*, Op. 100, No. 13
30   La tarentelle (Tarantella) from *25 Easy and Progressive Studies*, Op. 100, No. 20
32   Confidence from *18 Characteristic Studies*, Op. 109, No. 1
29   Berceuse (Lullaby) from *18 Characteristic Studies*, Op. 109, No. 7
34   Agitato from *18 Characteristic Studies*, Op. 109, No. 8

FRÉDÉRIC CHOPIN
36   Prélude in E minor, Op. 28, No. 4
37   Prélude in B minor, Op. 28, No. 6

EDVARD GRIEG
38   Arietta from *Lyric Pieces*, Op. 12, No. 1
42   Waltz in A minor from *Lyric Pieces*, Op. 12, No. 2
44   Album Leaf from *Lyric Pieces*, Op. 12, No. 7
39   Puck from *Lyric Pieces*, Op. 71, No. 3

CORNELIUS GURLITT
4   Hunting Song from *Albumleaves for the Young*, Op. 101, No. 19

STEPHEN HELLER
46   The Brook from *25 Melodious Etudes*, Op. 45, No. 1
48   The Avalanche from *25 Melodious Etudes*, Op. 45, No. 2
50   Sorrow and Joy from *25 Melodious Etudes*, Op. 45, No. 4

FRIEDRICH KUHLAU

Sonatina in C Major, Op. 55, No. 1
52   Allegro
53   Vivace

THEODOR KULLAK

56   On the Playground from *Scenes from Childhood*, Op. 62, No. 4
57   Grandmother Tells a Ghost Story from *Scenes from Childhood*, Op. 81, No. 3

FRANZ LISZT

58   Farewell
60   Gray Clouds

EDWARD MACDOWELL

62   To a Wild Rose from *Woodland Sketches*, Op. 51, No. 1

FELIX MENDELSSOHN

64   Song Without Words in A Major, Op. 19, No. 4
65   Song Without Words in E Major, Op. 30, No. 3

FRANZ SCHUBERT

66   Scherzo in B-flat Major from *2 Scherzos*, D. 593

ROBERT SCHUMANN

68   Von fremden Ländern und Menschen (About Strange Lands and People)
         from *Scenes from Childhood*, Op. 15, No. 1
69   Kleine Romanze (Little Romance) from *Album for the Young*, Op. 68, No. 19
70   Reiterstücke (The Horseman) from *Album for the Young*, Op. 68, No. 23
72   Nachklänge aus dem Theater (Echoes from the Theatre)
         from *Album for the Young*, Op. 68, No. 25
74   Fremder Mann (Strange Man) from *Album for the Young*, Op. 68, No. 29
77   Little Lullaby from *Albumleaves*, Op. 124, No. 6

PYOTR IL'YICH TCHAIKOVSKY

78   March of the Tin Soldiers from *Album for the Young*, Op. 39, No. 5
80   Mazurka in D minor from *Album for the Young*, Op. 39, No. 10
81   Russian Song from *Album for the Young*, Op. 39, No. 11
82   The Peasant Plays the Accordion from *Album for the Young*, Op. 39, No. 12
84   Sweet Dreams from *Album for the Young*, Op. 39, No. 21
86   The Organ Grinder from *Album for the Young*, Op. 39, No. 23

Hunting Song

from *Albumleaves for the Young*

Cornelius Gurlitt
Op. 101, No. 19

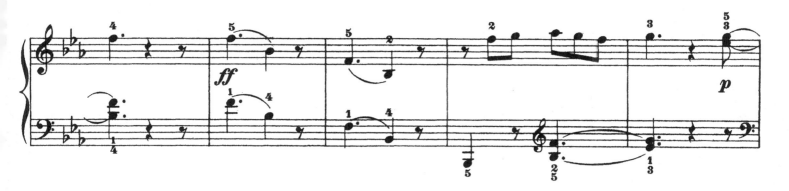

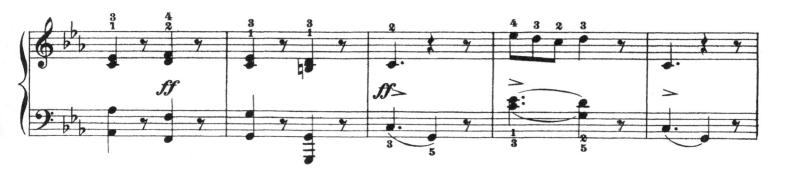

6

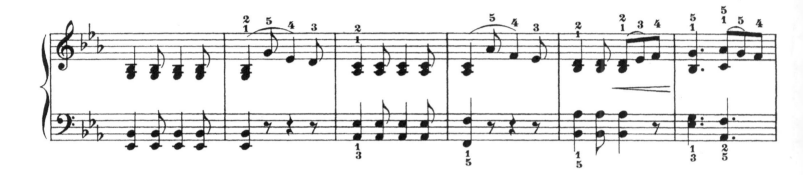

March
in G Major

Carl Philipp Emanuel Bach
BWV Appendix 124

Invention No. 1
in C Major

Johann Sebastian Bach
BWV 772

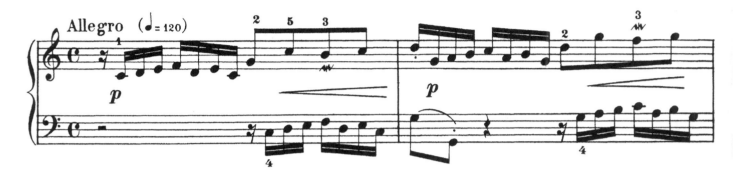

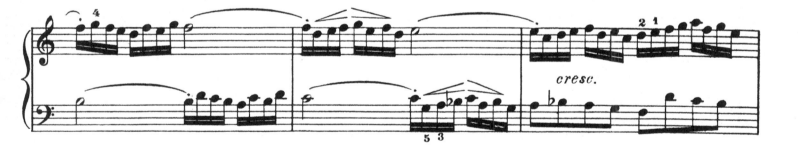

Invention No. 2
in C minor

Johann Sebastian Bach
BWV 773

Allegro moderato (♩=108)

Invention No. 4
in D minor

Johann Sebastian Bach
BWV 775

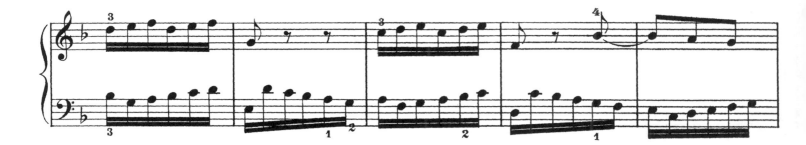

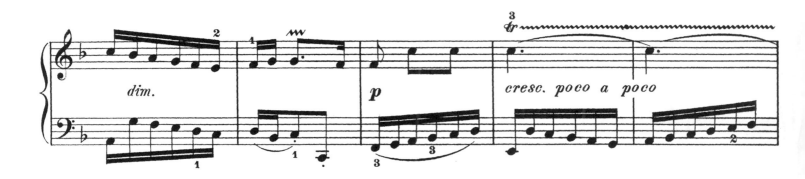

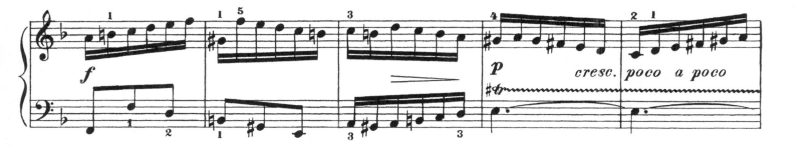

Invention No. 8
in F Major

Johann Sebastian Bach
BWV 779

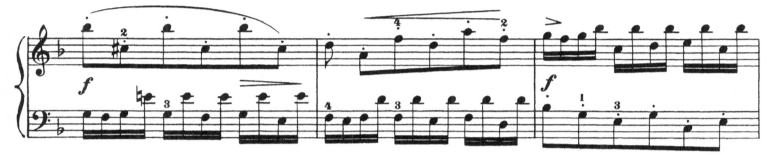

Prelude
in C Major
from *The Well-Tempered Clavier*, Book 1

Johann Sebastian Bach
BWV 846

All figures in the fingering which are set above the notes are intended, whether in inner or outer parts, for the right rand; whereas, the figures below the notes are for the left hand. This explanation will suffice to show, in doubtful cases, by which hand any note in the parts is to be played.

Prelude
in C minor

Johann Sebastian Bach
BWV 999

Con moto (♩=120)

Bourée

from Lute Suite No. 1 in E minor

Johann Sebastian Bach
BWV 996

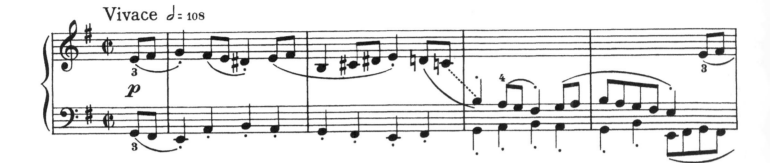

Six Variations on a Swiss Song

Ludwig van Beethoven
WoO 64

*) We call special attention to these thoroughly de-
lightful Variations because they are far too little known
and appreciated. They will be particularly welcome to
young pianists.
(a) By a comma we mark those points at which the

player ought, by lifting his hands a little earlier than
the note-value indicates, to bring out a rhythmical di-
vision.
(b) Proceed without interrupting the rhythm; and sim-
ilarly after Variations 1 and 3.

Minore

Poco sostenuto e doloroso ($\quad$ = 112)

Var. III

sempre **p** e legato

Maggiore

Tempo I un poco animato ($\quad$ =126)

Var. IV

legato

Ped. simile

Poco più tranquillo (♩ = 116)

Var. V

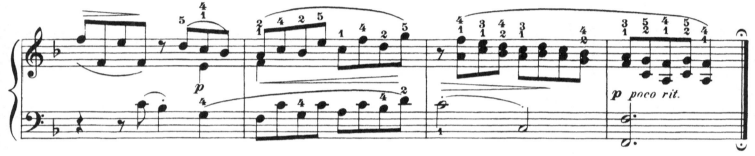

Con fuoco (♩ = 126)

Var. VI

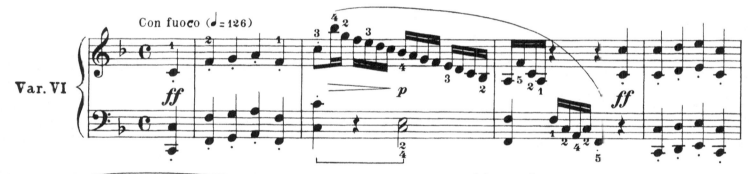

Coda

(a) 𝄢 or easier 𝄢

La chasse

(The Chase)

from *25 Easy and Progressive Studies*

Johann Friedrich Burgmüller
Op. 100, No. 9

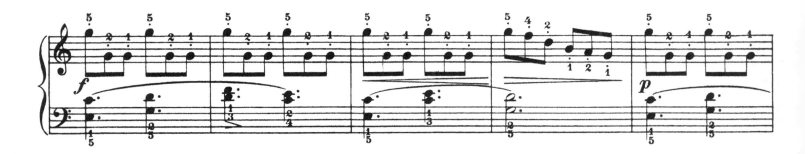

L'adieu
(The Farewell)
from *25 Easy and Progressive Studies*

Johann Friedrich Burgmüller
Op. 100, No. 12

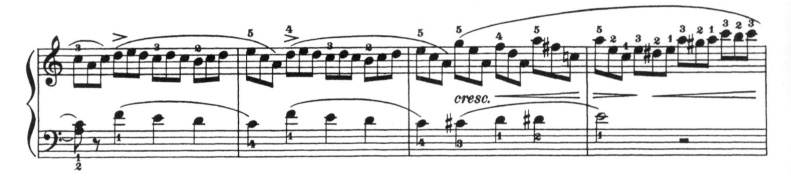

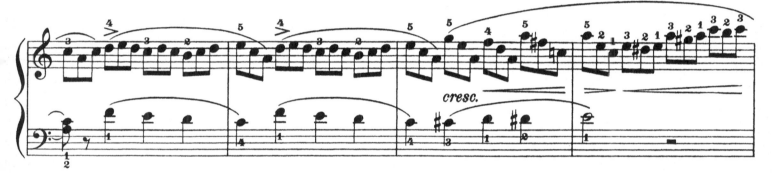

Consolation

from *25 Easy and Progressive Studies*

Johann Friedrich Burgmüller
Op. 100, No.13

Allegro moderato (♩=152)

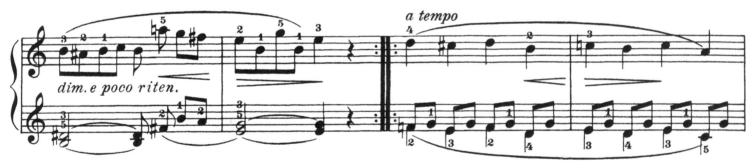

Berceuse

(Lullaby)

from *18 Characteristic Studies*

Johann Friedrich Burgmüller
Op. 109, No. 7

La tarentelle

(Tarantella)

from *25 Easy and Progressive Studies*

Johann Friedrich Burgmüller
Op. 100, No. 20

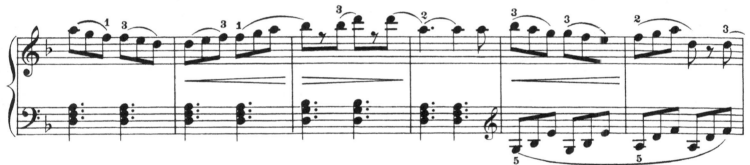

Confidence

from *18 Characteristic Studies*

Johann Friedrich Burgmüller
Op. 109, No. 1

Allegro non troppo ($\quad$ = 152)

Agitato

from *18 Characteristic Studies*

Johann Friedrich Burgmüller
Op. 109, No. 8

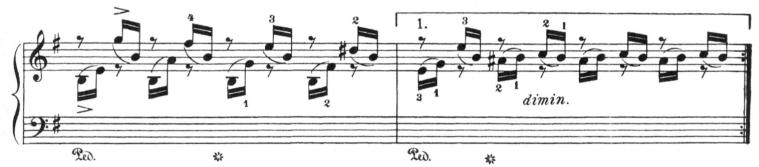

à J. C. Kessler

Prélude
in E minor

Frédéric Chopin
Op. 28, No. 4

à J. C. Kessler

Prélude
in B minor

Frédéric Chopin
Op. 28, No. 6

Lento assai

Arietta

from *Lyric Pieces*

Edvard Grieg
Op. 12, No. 1

Poco Andante e sostenuto

Puck

from *Lyric Pieces*

Edvard Grieg
Op. 71, No. 3

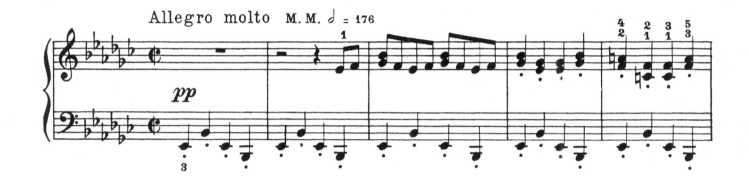

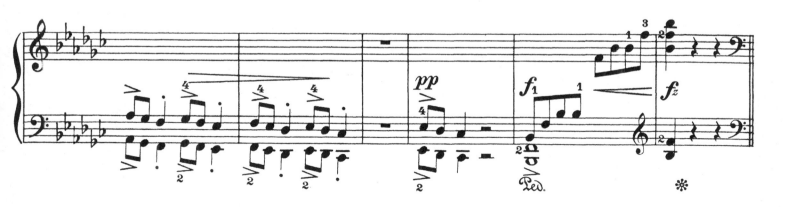

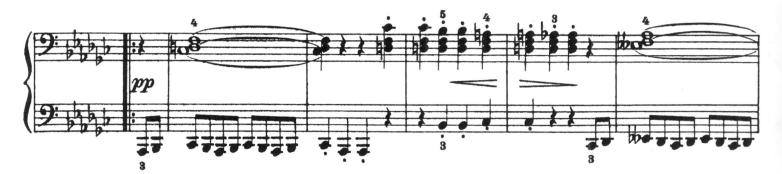

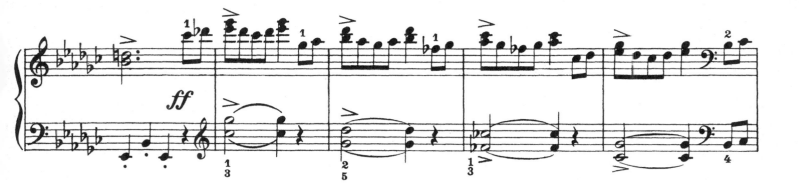
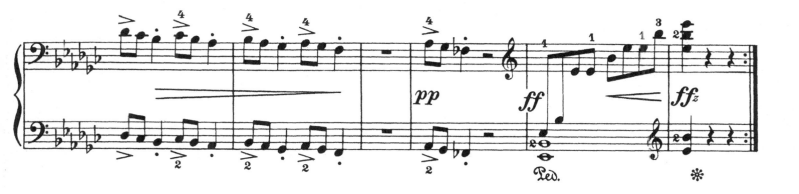

Waltz

in A minor
from *Lyric Pieces*

Edvard Grieg
Op. 12, No. 2

Coda

Album Leaf

from *Lyric Pieces*

Edvard Grieg
Op. 12, No. 7

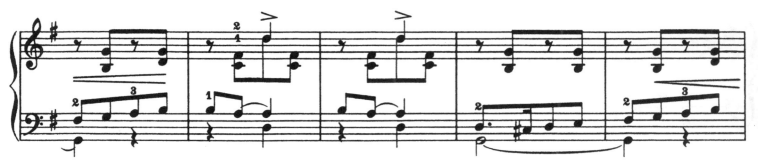

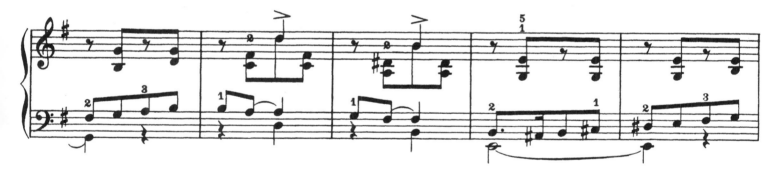

The Brook

from *25 Melodious Etudes*

Stephen Heller
Op. 45, No. 1

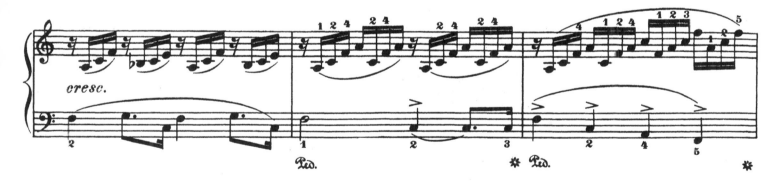

The Avalanche

from *25 Melodious Etudes*

Stephen Heller
Op. 45, No. 2

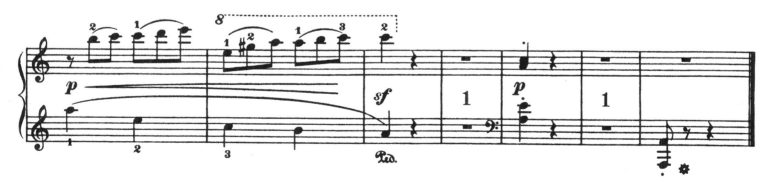

Sorrow and Joy

from *25 Melodious Etudes*

Stephen Heller
Op. 45, No. 4

Allegretto

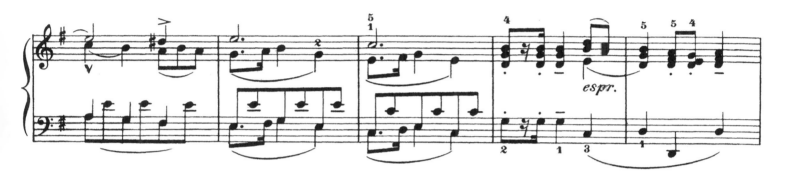

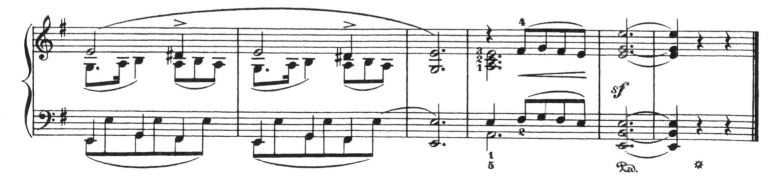

Sonatina
in C Major

Friedrich Kuhlau
Op. 55, No. 1

*) Remark: These small slurs indicate that the last bass-note in one measure should be carefully connected with the first bass-note in the next.

espressivo

dolce

p legato

On the Playground
from *Scenes from Childhood*

Theodor Kullak
Op. 62, No. 4

Allegro vivace

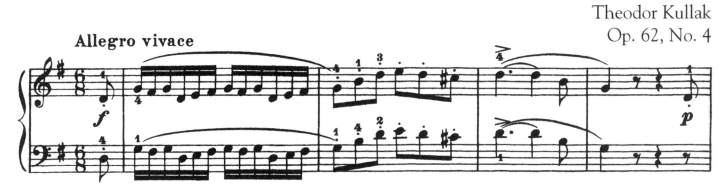

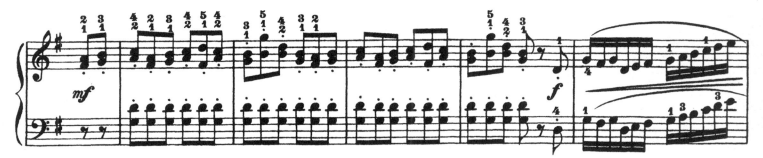

Grandmother Tells a Ghost Story

from *Scenes from Childhood*

Theodor Kullak
Op. 81, No. 3

to A. Siloti

Farewell*

Franz Liszt

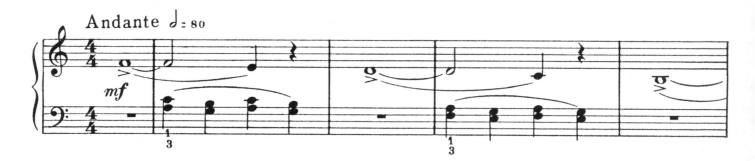

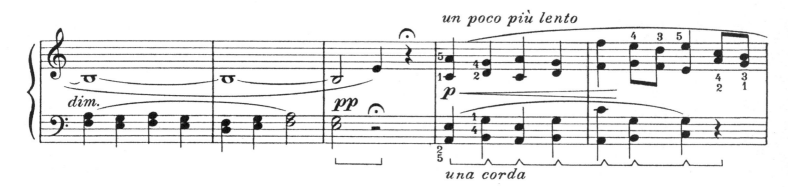

*Russian folk song

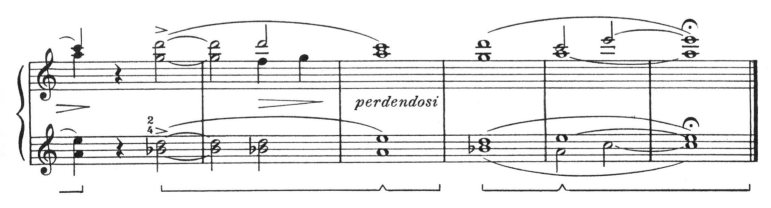

Gray Clouds

Franz Liszt

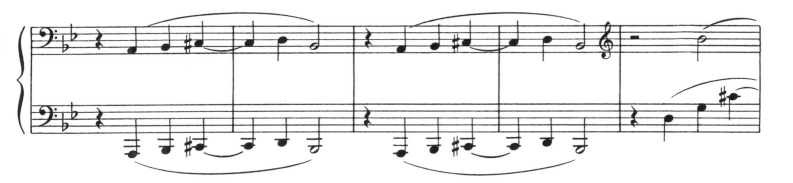

To a Wild Rose
from *Woodland Sketches*

Edward MacDowell
Op. 51, No. 1

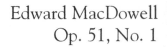

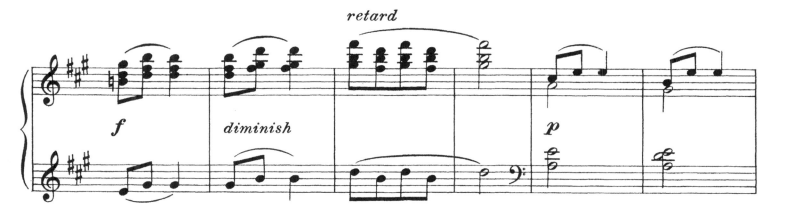

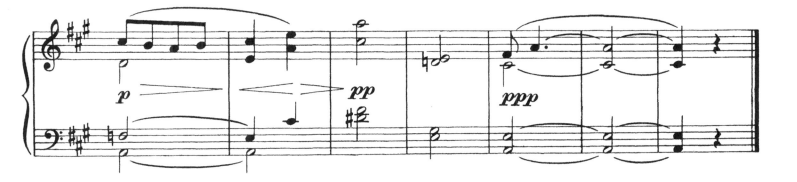

Song Without Words

in A Major

Felix Mendelssohn
Op. 19, No. 4

Song Without Words
in E Major

Felix Mendelssohn
Op. 30, No. 3

Scherzo
in B-flat Major
from *2 Scherzos*

Franz Schubert
D. 593

Trio

Scherzo D.C.

Von fremden Ländern und Menschen

(About Strange Lands and People)

from *Scenes from Childhood*

Robert Schumann
Op. 15, No. 1

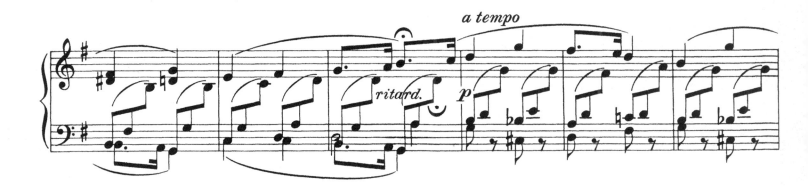

Kleine Romanze

(Little Romance)

from *Album for the Young*

Robert Schumann
Op. 68, No. 19

Reiterstücke

(The Horseman)

from *Album for the Young*

Robert Schumann
Op. 68, No. 23

Nachklänge aus dem Theater
(Echoes from the Theatre)
from *Album for the Young*

Robert Schumann
Op. 68, No. 25

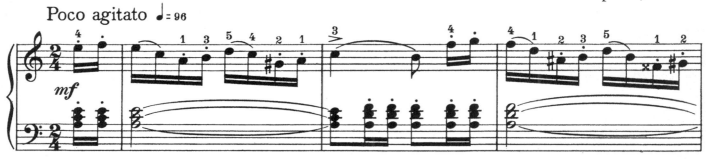

Fremder Mann

(Strange Man)

from *Album for the Young*

Robert Schumann
Op. 68, No. 29

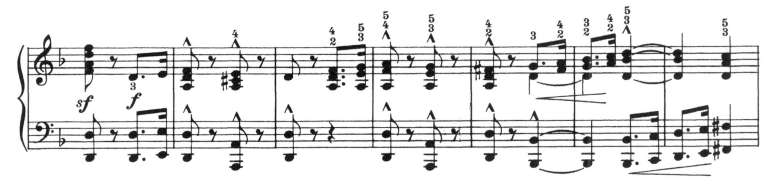

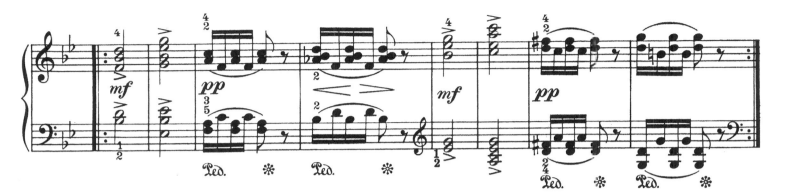

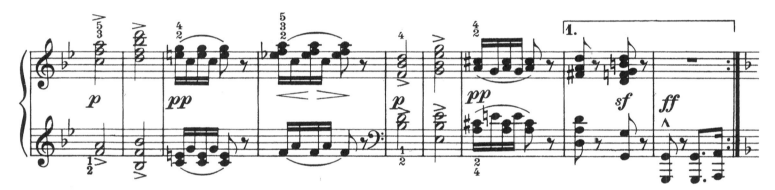

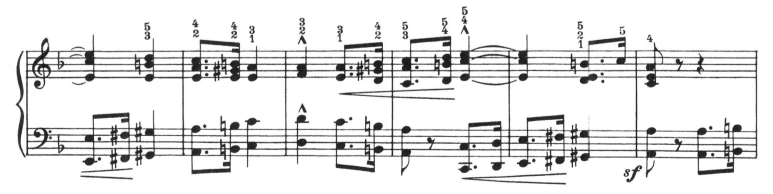

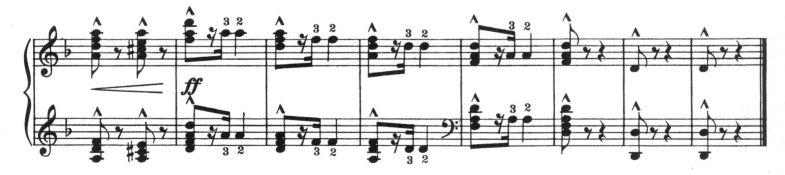

Little Lullaby

from *Albumleaves*

Robert Schumann
Op. 124, No. 6

March of the Tin Soldiers

from *Album for the Young*

Pyotr Il'yich Tchaikovsky
Op. 39, No. 5

Tempo di Marcia

Mazurka
in D minor
from *Album for the Young*

Pyotr Il'yich Tchaikovsky
Op. 39, No. 10

Tempo di Mazurka

Russian Song
from *Album for the Young*

Pyotr Il'yich Tchaikovsky
Op. 39, No. 11

The Peasant Plays the Accordion

from *Album for the Young*

Pyotr Il'yich Tchaikovsky
Op. 39, No. 12

Sweet Dreams
from *Album for the Young*

Pyotr Il'yich Tchaikovsky
Op. 39, No. 21

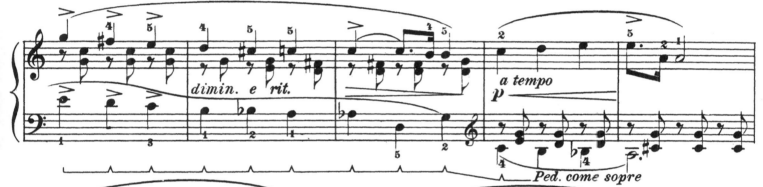

The Organ Grinder

from *Album for the Young*

Pyotr Il'yich Tchaikovsky
Op. 39, No. 23